Mom, I Want to Know You Better

A Mother's Guided Keepsake Journal to Share Her Memories and Life

Producer & International Distributor
eBookPro Publishing
www.ebook-pro.com

Mom, I Want to Know You Better
Made Easy Press

Copyright © 2022 Made Easy Press

All rights reserved; No parts of this book may be reproduced or transmitted in any form or by any means, electronic or mechanical, including photocopying, recording, taping, or by any information retrieval system, without the author's explicit permission in writing.

Written by Dani Silas
Design by Natalie Lukatsky

Contact: agency@ebook-pro.com

Contents

A Letter to My Mom 9

About Me 13

Our Family Tree 14

The Year I Was Born 16

Family 20

Early Life and Childhood 28

Growing Up 38

Work 44

Love and Marriage 50

Motherhood 66

Who I Am Now 74

My Favorites 76

Would You Rather 80

Top 5 82

Looking Back 90

My Wishes for You 96

A Letter to My Dear Child 99

"Once you're a mom, you're always a mom. It's like riding a bike, you never forget."

– Taraji P. Henson

"My mother was my role model before I even knew what that word was."

— Lisa Leslie

This Book Belongs To...

....

A Letter to My Mom

Sign your name

> "Being a mama can be tough, but always remember in the eyes of your child, no one does it better than you."
>
> – Unknown

"I believe the choice to become a mother is the choice to become one of the greatest spiritual teachers there is."

– Oprah

About Me

Full Name

Date of Birth

Zodiac Sign

Height

Hair Color

Eye Color

Distinguishing Marks

Languages I speak

Our Family Tree

_____   _____
My Great-Grandfather   **My Great-Grandfather**

_____   _____
My Great-Grandmother   **My Great-Grandmother**

_____   _____
My Grandmother   **My Grandfather**

_____
My Mother

_____   _____   _____
Me   **My Sibling**   **My Sibling**

My Great-Grandfather

My Great-Grandfather

My Great-Grandmother

My Great-Grandmother

My Grandmother

My Grandfather

My Father

My Sibling

My Sibling

My Sibling

The Year I Was Born...

Who was the leader of your country?
_____

Who was the mayor of your city?
_____

Which celebrities were born in the same year?
_____
_____
_____

Were there any big scientific discoveries?
_____
_____
_____

Were there any important inventions?
_____
_____
_____

Were there any important events happening in the world?

___

Which memorable movies came out?

___

Did anyone famous pass away?

___

What was the price of a carton of milk?

Picture Gallery

Childhood Photo

Place your childhood photo here

Family Photo

Place your family photo here

Family

What are your parents' names?

_____

How old were they when you were born?

_____

What were their professions?

_____

_____

Who do you take after most in looks?

_____

_____

Which physical attributes do you share?

_____

_____

Who do you take after most in personality?

_____

_____

_____

Which qualities or attributes do you share?

_____

_____

_____

What are your grandparents' names?

_____

_____

Did you know them?

_____

_____

Did your grandparents live close by? How often did you see them?

_____

_____

Do you have any treasured memories with your grandparents?

_____

_____

_____

_____

How many siblings do you have?

_____

What are their names?

_____

Where are you in order of birth?

_____

Which sibling looks most similar to you?

_____

Which sibling is most like you in personality?

_____

How was your relationship with your siblings growing up?

_____

_____

Has your relationship with your siblings changed throughout your life? If so, in what way?

_____

_____

What is your favorite childhood memory with your siblings?

_____

_____

What did you like to do together when you were younger?

_____

_____

Do you have any brothers-or-sisters-in-law? What are their names?

_____

_____

How did they and your siblings meet?

_____

_____

Do you have any nieces and nephews? What are their names?

_____

_____

How old were you when your first niece or nephew was born?

_____

Did you ever babysit or look after them?

_____

_____

Did you see them often when they were children?

_____

What special memories do you have with your nieces and nephews?

_____

_____

Do you have any aunts and uncles? What are their names?

_____

_____

How is your relationship with your aunts and uncles?

_____
_____
_____

Do you have any cousins? What are their names?

_____
_____

Did you grow up close by to any of your cousins?

_____
_____
_____

Are there any cousins you have a particularly close relationship with?

_____
_____
_____

What are some favorite memories with your extended family?

_____
_____
_____
_____

Share a Family Recipe

_____

Ingredients:

_____
_____
_____
_____

Instructions:

_____
_____
_____
_____
_____
_____
_____
_____
_____
_____

"I love my mother and father. The older I get, the more I value everything that they gave me."

– Liev Schreiber

"There is no leadership more important than parenthood."

– Sheri L. Dew

Early Life and Childhood
Birth

Where were you born?

_____

How close to your due date were you born?

_____

How much did you weigh at birth?

_____

What was your length?

_____

What was the full name you were given?

_____

_____

Were you named after anyone? If so, whom?

_____

_____

Did you have a nickname as a baby?

_____

Have you always liked your name?

_____

_____

Were you the firstborn or did you have siblings?

_____

How did your family celebrate your birth?

_____

_____

_____

What stories does your family tell about your birth?

_____

_____

_____

_____

How did your parents describe you as a baby?

_____

_____

_____

Firsts

When did you first grab a toy?

___

When did you first smile?

___

When did you first laugh?

___

When did you first roll over?

___

When did you first sit up unsupported?

___

When did you first crawl?

___

When did you first stand?

___

When did you first walk?

___

When did you say your first word?

___

What was your first word?

___

What was the first solid food you ate?

___

Childhood

What is your earliest memory?

___

___

___

Did you have a nickname as a child?

___

At what age did you first go to kindergarten? Do you remember anything about it?

___

___

___

Who were your best friends as a small child?

___

Where did you go to elementary school?

___

Who were your first school friends?

_____

_____

What was the name of your first-grade teacher? Did you like him/her?

_____

What was your favorite subject in elementary school?

_____

What was your least favorite subject?

_____

What did you excel at?

_____

What did you like to do during recess?

_____

Did you play any sports or instruments?

_____

_____

Which other hobbies did you have as a child?

_____

_____

What did your childhood room look like? Did you share with anyone?

_____
_____
_____

What is your favorite memory from elementary school?

_____
_____
_____
_____

Who was your favorite teacher at school?

_____
_____

How did you celebrate your early birthdays?

_____
_____
_____
_____

What is your favorite birthday memory?

_____
_____
_____
_____

What is your favorite childhood holiday memory?

_____
_____
_____
_____

Where did your family go on vacations?

_____
_____
_____
_____

Did your family have any pets? What were their names? Who was in charge of them?

_____
_____
_____
_____

What were you afraid of as a child?

What did you most love to do?

What did you most love to eat?

Which family members were you particularly close with?

"A mother's arms are made of tenderness and children sleep soundly in them."

– Victor Hugo

"A child's first teacher is its mother."

– Peng Liyuan

Growing Up

Where did you go to middle school?

___

Where did you go to high school?

___

What was your favorite subject in high school?

___

What was your least favorite subject?

___

Who was your favorite teacher? What do you remember about him/her?

___

___

___

Which extracurricular activities did you participate in?

___

___

___

Did your school have a mascot or school colors? What were they?

___

___

Did you have a school uniform? What did it look like?

_____

_____

Did you play any sports or instruments in high school?

_____

_____

_____

What did you like to do outside of school?

_____

_____

_____

Who were your best friends as a teenager?

_____

_____

What did you like to do with your friends?

_____

_____

_____

Did you go on dates in high school?

_____

_____

Did you have a curfew?

_____

Did your parents give you an allowance? If so, how much was it?

_____

Did you have any chores around the house? Which ones?

_____

_____

Did you enjoy your chores?

_____

When did you get your driver's license?

_____

How many times did you take the driver's test before you passed?

_____

Who helped you learn to drive?

_____

Did you like driving?

_____

Did you have your own car as a teenager?

_____

What was your relationship with your family like as a teenager?

_____

_____

_____

What kind of clothes were in style when you were a teen?

_____

_____

Is there a fashion style from your childhood that you particularly miss?

_____

_____

What kind of music was popular then?

_____

_____

Was there anything you didn't appreciate as a teen but can see the value of today?

_____

_____

What did you like to do on weekends?

_____

_____

Who was your favorite musician?

_____

_____

Did you ever see any musicians live in concert?

_____

Did you ever attend a music festival?

How did you celebrate your birthday in your teen years?

Did you have a sweet sixteen / quinceanera / bar/bat mitzvah, or some other special celebration? How did you celebrate it?

Which subjects did you take in high school?

How did you do on your final exams?

Did you acquire a high school diploma?

Did you have a graduation ceremony?

_____

How was it?

_____

_____

_____

_____

Did you attend prom?

_____

Where was it?

_____

Did you enjoy it?

_____

_____

_____

_____

Who did you go with?

_____

_____

What did you wear?

_____

_____

Work

What was your very first job?

_____

_____

How much did it pay?

_____

How did you get it?

_____

_____

Did you enjoy the work?

_____

What do you feel like you learned from that first job?

_____

_____

_____

Which jobs did you have as a teenager?

_____

_____

_____

_____

Did you ever have an unpaid temp job? What was it?

_____

_____

What was your dream job growing up?

_____

What was the first job you held where you felt truly independent?

_____

What was the shortest job you ever held?

_____

What was the longest job you ever held?

_____

What was your favorite job?

_____

What were your work hours most of your life?

_____

Did you work as a salaried employee or were you self-employed?

_____

Who was your favorite boss?

_____

_____

Who was your least favorite boss?

_____
_____

Did you have coworkers who became good friends?

_____
_____
_____

Did you have any coworkers you didn't get along with? Why?

_____
_____
_____

When interviewing for a job, what things was it important to you to say about yourself?

_____
_____
_____
_____

Share a Family Recipe

_____

Ingredients:

_____
_____
_____
_____

Instructions:

_____
_____
_____
_____
_____
_____
_____
_____
_____
_____

"The best place to cry is on a mother's arms."

– Jodi Picoult

"Life doesn't come with a manual, it comes with a mother."

– Unknown

Love and Marriage
Young Love and Dating

Who was your first ever crush? Did they know or was it a secret?

_____

_____

Who did you go on your first date with?

_____

Where did you go and what did you do?

_____

_____

_____

How old were you?

_____

How did you meet?

_____

Who was your first kiss?

_____

Where did it happen?

_____

_____

With whom did you first fall in love?

_____

How did the two of you meet?

_____

_____

What was your first impression of your current partner?

_____

_____

How did the two of you meet and where?

_____

_____

Did you start dating right away or were you friends first?

_____

_____

What did you like to do most while you were going out?

_____

_____

Do you believe in soul mates?

_____

_____

Picture Gallery

Couple Photo

Place your couple photo here

Wedding Photo

Place your wedding photo here

Wedding

Did you have a proposal? Where did it happen and how?

_____
_____
_____
_____
_____

What did the engagement ring look like?

_____
_____

How did you know you wanted to marry your partner?

_____
_____
_____
_____

How long had you been together before you got engaged?

_____
_____

How did you celebrate your engagement?

_____
_____
_____
_____

Who did you tell first, and how?

_____
_____
_____
_____

How long was your engagement?

_____
_____

Did you enjoy planning the wedding? Who helped with the arrangements?

_____
_____

When did you get married?

_____

Where was the ceremony held?

_____

Did you have a party? How did you celebrate your marriage?

_____
_____
_____
_____

Did you have bridesmaids or groomsmen? If so, who were they?

_____
_____

What did they wear?

_____
_____

Did you have flower girls or ring bearers? If so, who were they?

_____
_____

What did they wear?

_____
_____

Who married you?

_____
_____

Did you write your own vows? What did they say?

_____
_____
_____
_____

What did you wear to your wedding?

_____
_____
_____

Were there any funny moments on your wedding day?

_____
_____
_____
_____
_____

Did you have a cake?

_____
_____

Who gave speeches?

_____
_____

Did you receive any particularly memorable wedding gifts?

_____
_____
_____

Do you have any keepsakes from the wedding?

_____
_____
_____

Did you go on a honeymoon? If so, where too? Did you enjoy it?

_____
_____
_____
_____
_____
_____

Have you been married more than once? If so, to whom?

_____
_____
_____
_____
_____
_____

Married Life

Did being married feel different in any way than before?

Do you wear a wedding ring? If so, what does it look like?

What are your favorite attributes in your partner?

What are their favorite attributes in you?

How do you celebrate your anniversaries?

_____
_____
_____
_____

What are some traditions you and your partner have?

_____
_____
_____
_____
_____
_____

Have you ever had troubles in your marriage? How did you solve them?

_____
_____
_____
_____
_____
_____
_____

What do you think are the foundations of a successful marriage?

What is the best advice you can give to married couples?

Do you have a favorite romantic memory?

_____
_____
_____
_____
_____
_____
_____
_____
_____

How do you feel your marriage was influenced by marriages of other people close to you?

_____
_____
_____
_____
_____
_____
_____

Share a Family Recipe

_____

Ingredients:

_____
_____
_____
_____

Instructions:

_____
_____
_____
_____
_____
_____
_____
_____
_____
_____

"Children are the anchors that hold a mother to life."

– Sophocles

"The most important thing in the world is family and love."

– John Wooden

Motherhood

How old were you when you first became a mother?
_____

How many children do you have?
_____

What are their names?
_____
_____

Were your children named after anyone? If so, whom?
_____
_____
_____

What did it feel like to become a mother?
_____
_____
_____

Did you try for a long time before you had children? Was it expected or unexpected?
_____
_____
_____

How were your pregnancies?

_____

_____

_____

How were your birth experiences?

_____

_____

_____

_____

Did you read any books to prepare for motherhood? If so, which?

_____

_____

_____

For each of your children, name your favorite attribute of theirs

_____

_____

_____

_____

What is the best part of being a mother?

_____

_____

_____

What is the most difficult part of being a mother?

_____
_____
_____
_____

Who helped you most in your early motherhood days?

_____

Were the grandparents involved in the early days? How did they help?

_____
_____

What influences did you have in raising your children?

_____
_____
_____

Did you and your partner divide responsibilities between you when your children were young?

_____
_____
_____

Did you take time off work when your children were born?

_____
_____

Did having children impact your career? If so, how?

_____

_____

What has motherhood taught you?

_____

_____

_____

_____

_____

Did you have any special traditions with your children?

_____

_____

_____

_____

Did you have a favorite book to read them or lullaby song to sing them?

_____

_____

_____

What was your kids' bedtime routine?

_____

_____

_____

What do your children call you?

What advice would you give new mothers?

What would you do differently if you could do it all again?

Share a Family Recipe

_____

Ingredients:

_____
_____
_____
_____

Instructions:

_____
_____
_____
_____
_____
_____
_____
_____
_____
_____

Picture Gallery

Photo with Your Children

Place a photo with your children here

Family Photo

Place your family photo here

Who I Am Now

My age

___

Where I live

___

My favorite way to spend the day

___

___

___

My hobbies

___

___

___

My best friends

___

___

Things that make me happy

___

___

___

The places I have lived:

_____
_____
_____

The places I have traveled:

_____
_____
_____
_____
_____

My fondest memories:

_____
_____
_____
_____
_____
_____
_____

My greatest achievements:

_____
_____
_____
_____
_____

My Favorites

Color:

___

Meal:

___

Restaurant:

___

Cold drink:

___

Hot drink:

___

Holiday:

___

Book:

___

Movie:

___

TV show:

_____

Dessert:

_____

Sport:

_____

Actor:

_____

Board or card game:

_____

Musician:

_____

Animal:

_____

Outfit:

_____

"*A mother always has to think twice, once for herself and once for her child.*"

– Sophia Loren

"My mother's love has always been a sustaining force for our family."

– Michelle Obama

Would You Rather

Cook ☐ OR Clean ☐	Cats ☐ OR Dogs ☐
Movie ☐ OR TV show ☐	Fancy clothes ☐ OR Pajamas ☐
Travel by plane ☐ OR Travel by boat ☐	Endless money ☐ OR Endless time ☐
Sing ☐ OR Dance ☐	Bath ☐ OR Shower ☐
Coffee ☐ OR Tea ☐	Beach vacation ☐ OR Sightseeing ☐

Would You Rather

Winter ☐ OR Summer ☐

Sushi ☐ OR Hamburger ☐

Read ☐ OR Write ☐

Camping ☐ OR Hotel ☐

Zoo ☐ OR Botanical garden ☐

Picnic ☐ OR Restaurant ☐

Hiking ☐ OR Skiing ☐

Stay up late ☐ OR Get up early ☐

Drive ☐ OR Be driven ☐

Be able to fly ☐ OR Read minds ☐

Top 5

Your top 5 travel destinations:

1. _____

2. _____

3. _____

4. _____

5. _____

Your top 5 movies:

1. _____

2. _____

3. _____

4. _____

5. _____

Your top 5 books:

1. _____

2. _____

3. _____

4. _____

5. _____

Your top 5 jobs:

1. _____

2. _____

3. _____

4. _____

5. _____

Your top 5 best presents you received:

1. _____

2. _____

3. _____

4. _____

5. _____

Your top 5 meals you ever ate:

1. _____

2. _____

3. _____

4. _____

5. _____

Your top 5 vacations:

1. _____

2. _____

3. _____

4. _____

5. _____

Your top 5 most important moments:

1. _____

2. _____

3. _____

4. _____

5. _____

Your top 5 biggest successes:

1. _____

2. _____

3. _____

4. _____

5. _____

Your top 5 favorite attributes in people:

1. _____

2. _____

3. _____

4. _____

5. _____

Your top 5 funny memories:

1. _____

2. _____

3. _____

4. _____

5. _____

Your top 5 best tips for life:

1. _____

2. _____

3. _____

4. _____

5. _____

"Mothers hold their children's hands for a short while, but their hearts forever."

– Unknown

"Mother's love is peace. It need not be acquired, it need not be deserved."

– Erich Fromm

Looking Back

What is your favorite inspirational quote?

_____

_____

_____

What do you think everyone should experience at least once in a lifetime?

_____

_____

_____

Do you have any serious regrets? What are they?

_____

_____

_____

What would you want to tell your younger self today?

_____

_____

_____

_____

_____

_____

What life experience has impacted you the most?

Do you believe in miracles? Have you ever experienced one?

How do you find inner strength in times of struggle?

What is the one thing that always makes you feel better when you're sad?

What fears have you had and how have you overcome them?

Where were you during the 9/11 attacks?

What do you think is the most important foundation in a friendship?

What do you consider to be a waste of money or time?

What is your worst habit?

_____

_____

What do you think your three best qualities are?

_____

_____

_____

What do you think your three worst qualities are?

_____

_____

_____

Which things make you feel stressed?

_____

_____

_____

What are you most grateful for?

_____

_____

_____

_____

_____

> "Motherhood is the greatest thing and the hardest thing."
>
> – Ricki Lake

"Sometimes the strength of motherhood is greater than natural laws."

– Barbara Kingsolver

My Wishes for You

Something I hope you experience in your lifetime

_____
_____
_____
_____

I wish you a relationship that…

_____
_____
_____
_____

I wish you a family that…

_____
_____
_____
_____

I wish you memories that…

_____
_____
_____
_____
_____

I wish you a career that…

_____
_____
_____
_____

I wish you a life that…

_____
_____
_____
_____

In 10 years, I hope you…

_____
_____
_____
_____

My biggest dreams for you…

_____
_____
_____
_____

To my dear Child,

Sign your name

Share a Family Recipe

_____

Ingredients:

_____
_____
_____
_____

Instructions:

_____
_____
_____
_____
_____
_____
_____
_____
_____
_____

Notes

Notes

"**Motherhood changes everything.**"

– Ricki Lake

"A mother's happiness is like a beacon."

– Honore de Balzac

Thank You!

We hope you enjoyed this book and that it was everything you expected it to be.

Our mission is to bring families together and help you make special memories with your loved ones which they can cherish forever.

To keep bringing love and light to the world, we would love it if you could take a minute to leave a positive review on Amazon so that other people can enjoy this journal, just as you have.

www.ingramcontent.com/pod-product-compliance
Lightning Source LLC
LaVergne TN
LVHW081534070526
838199LV00006B/356